Making a Better Confession

Con O'Connell, O.F.M.

Liguori

Imprimi Potest:
James Shea, CSsR
Provincial, St. Louis Province
The Redemptorists

Imprimatur:
+Paul Zipfel, V.G.
Auxiliary Bishop, Archdiocese of St. Louis

ISBN 978-0-89243-863-1

Cover design by Myra Roth
Cover and page 32 photograph by Anthony F. Chiffolo
Photograph on page 9, 14, and 31 by SuperStock

First published by Redemptorist Publications
Alphonsus House Chawton Alton Hampshire, England

To order, call 800-325-9521 or visit Liguori.org

CONTENTS

*"It's a long time since
my last confession."*

*"I can never think of
anything much to tell."*

*"I always seem to say
the same old things."*

*"I don't really feel
any better afterward."*

"It's just become routine."

*"I wish I could find a way
of making a better confession."*

Many of us are unhappy about confession. And it doesn't seem to have much to do with giving the sacrament other names, as the *Catechism of the Catholic Church* does (CCC 1423-1424), with being able to choose between the traditional confessional and face to face, or with celebrating this sacrament individually or in common with others (CCC 1480-1484).

One big stumbling block is the way we examine our conscience. Very often we don't seem to be able to find anything worth confessing; or we come up with the same old faults time after time. The root of the problem is that we think we have to examine our conscience on our own instead of with the help of our Lord Jesus and his Holy Spirit.

We don't really know ourselves very well. We all have blind spots. We are all forgetful. But our Lord Jesus knows each one of us through and through. He loves us as we are: not as we could be or as we might be some day, but as we are now.

If we try to examine our conscience on our own, we run the risk of seeing things only from our own point of view. We misjudge our faults and weaknesses and even ignore some of them altogether. We can also get sick and tired of seeing the same old bad habits still there after all our good resolutions, and there is a strong temptation just to give up. Or we can go to the other extreme. Because we're only skimming the surface, we can kid ourselves that we're not really too bad after all. So we become complacent and rather pleased with ourselves.

Surely, then, it's common sense always to examine our conscience in our Lord's presence and under his direction (CCC 1454).

Going it alone leads to another reason for disappointing confessions: telling the symptoms instead of the sin. If we felt feverish and had a skin rash and a coated tongue, we'd expect the doctor to diagnose what was causing these symptoms and to treat the underlying sickness. When we examine our conscience on our own, we often don't go far enough in our diagnosis. We only look at the symptoms. We confess as sins what are really the symptoms of a deep and hidden soul-sickness: a constant attitude of self-interest that has trapped us in habits of self-centered behavior or a persistent weakness (CCC 1849–1850, 1505).

It is these deep-down attitudes that lie at the root of our symptoms—sins that we must ask Jesus to unmask. It is these we should bring before him and his Spirit in confession (CCC 1420-21, 1425-1433, 1440-1448).

Some wise person has said, "You'll never get the right answers if you're asking the wrong questions." How can we ask the right questions on our own? When we open the eyes of our mind to Jesus present in us and put ourselves in his care and under his direction, he will examine our conscience with us. He and the Holy Spirit will lead us to the right questions and the right answers.

The Lord be with you.

In the Lord's presence
(CCC 2665-68, 2670)

Jesus is with you.
Enter into the still center of yourself.
Become aware of him there.
Center your attention and your love on him.
Never mind about distracting sounds or feelings
or thoughts; keep coming back to him.
Your attention may wander but your love for him
stays.
Let your mind be in tune with his mind.
Take time to be calm and still in his company
(CCC 2709-2712).

Prayerfully ponder
the psalmist's words:

O Lord, you search me and you know me, / you know my resting and my rising, you discern my purpose from afar. / You mark when I walk or lie down, all my ways lie open to you.

Before ever a word is on my tongue / you know it, O Lord, through and through. Behind and before you besiege me, / your hand ever laid upon me. Too wonderful for me, this knowledge, / too high, beyond my reach.

O where can I go from your spirit, / or where can I flee from your face? If I climb the heavens, you are there. / If I lie in the grave, you are there.

If I take the wings of the dawn / and dwell at the sea's furthest end, even there your hand...would hold me fast.

If I say: "Let the darkness hide me / and the light around me be night," even darkness is not dark for you / and the night is as clear as the day.

For it was you who created my being, / knit me together in my mother's womb. I thank you for the wonder of my being, / for the wonders of all your creation.

Already you knew my soul, / my body held no secret from you when I was being fashioned in secret / and moulded in the depths of the earth.

Your eyes saw all my actions, / they were all of them written in your book; every one of my days was decreed / before one of them came into being.

To me, how mysterious your thoughts, / the sum of them not to be numbered! If I count them, they are more than the sand; to finish, I must be eternal, like you....

O search me, God, and know my heart. / O test me and know my thoughts. See that I follow not the wrong path / and lead me in the path of life eternal.

Psalm 138 (139):1-18,23-24

Then, taking your time, say to him in your own words or in these words:

Lord Jesus,
Open my mind and my heart to your
Holy Spirit.
Show me where I am failing to love your heavenly Father.
Show me where I am failing to love you,
failing to accept you as my savior,
failing to seek you and yield to you as my Lord.
Show me where I am failing
to love the Holy Spirit,
failing to be open
and to be led by Wisdom and Love.

Lord Jesus,
Show me where I am failing to love any one of
your brothers or sisters as you love me.
Show me where I am failing to love myself
as you love me.
Show me where I am putting myself before God.

Show me where I am seeking my own desires at the expense of a brother or sister.

Your power finds its strength in my weakness; without you I can do nothing.

Recall the words of Scripture:

"The LORD will fight for you, and you have only to keep still."

Exodus 14:14

My relationship with God

Addressing your thoughts to Jesus and yourself together, ask yourself and him:

Am I faithful to daily prayer? (CCC 2659-60).
If not, what is my attitude to God that allows me to neglect prayer?
Confess this attitude and examples of it.

Am I faithful to Mass? (CCC 1341-44, 2177-82).
If not, why not? What is my attitude to God that allows this to happen?
Confess this attitude and instances of it.

Am I going to Mass or saying my prayers as a duty and no more? Why do I give God the bare minimum?
Confess this attitude.

When I am distracted at Mass is it because I am making other things more important to me than God?
If so, confess—not just the distractions but the cause.

Ask yourself and our Lord further questions:

Do I trust God's loving care for me? How do I show this trust?
Do I make time to read Scripture, that I may know and hear Jesus and his Father? (CCC 2653-54).
Do I really try to seek God's will, not mine, in prayer?

Am I angry with, or afraid of, God?
Tell our Lord so, and hand such feelings over to him.

My relationship with those nearest to me

(CCC 2204-08, 2212-2231,1823,1889, 2196)

Ask yourself and our Lord:

Have I failed to respect any family member or friend? If so, why?
Confess the answer and the disrespect.

Have I failed to accept anyone just as he or she is? If so, why?
Confess the answer and the unacceptance.

Have I been patient with another's differences from me? If not, why not?
Confess the answer and the impatience, the domination, the manipulation.

Have I been tolerant with another's shortcomings? If not, why not?
Confess the answer and the intolerance.

Have I been sensitive to another's needs and weaknesses? If not, why not?
Confess the answer and the lack of sensitivity.

Am I refusing to forgive anyone, Lord, when you have forgiven me?

Am I nursing a grudge? If so, why?
Confess the answer.

Do I criticize and find fault? If so, why?
Confess the answer.

Do I show positive acts of kindness to others? If not, why not?
Confess the answer.

In the sight of the Lord

Bring each one of those nearest to you in your life, one by one, into your mind and heart in the presence of the Lord.

Ask him to let you see that person through his eyes and to show you what attitudes he wants you to have toward that person.

Ask him what he wants you to do for that person.

Ask him to show you if you are an obstacle to the Father's plan of love for any one of those who are nearest to you.

Take time to reflect on this in the Lord's presence and ask him for his help and healing.

Confess whatever may be revealed to you as being a stumbling block in someone's way to God.

My relationship
with everyone

**Now turn toward all people.
Ask yourself and the Lord in his presence**
(CCC 1928-42):

Do I despise any group of people?
If so, why?
Confess the answer and the disdain.

Do I discriminate against any group or individual
because of race, religion, nationality, politics, age,
profession, gender, any other reason?
If so, confess the answer.

Do I consider any group or individual inferior to
me? If so, why?
Confess the answer.

When someone has needed me, have I refused to
help? If so, why?
Confess the answer and the refusal.

Lord Jesus, you prayed that all who believe in you might be one. Do I pray for this? If not, why not? (CCC 820-22).
Confess the answer.

If so, what else do I do for Christian unity? If I do little or nothing, why not?
Confess the answer.

Now ask the Lord and yourself the same kinds of questions found on pages 17 through 19.

Lord Jesus,
You have said, "For if you love those who love you, what reward do you have? Do not even the tax collectors do the same? And if you greet only your brothers and sisters, what more are you doing than others? Do not even the [pagans] do the same?" (Matthew 5:46-47).

Show me where I am settling for loving like a pagan, Lord.

My relationship with God's other creatures

Ask yourself and our Lord:

Have I spoiled any part of creation? If so, why?
(CCC 2415).
Confess the answer and examples.

Have I abused animals by cruelty or neglect?
(CCC 2416-18).
If so, confess it.

Have I been wasteful?
If so, confess it.

Am I too fond of money? of material things?
(CCC 2551-2557).
If so, confess it.

Do I act as though everything I have is mine to do
with what I like? If so, why?
Confess the attitude and examples.

Am I open-handed and generous? or tight-fisted and mean? If the latter, why?
Confess the answer and examples.

Do I drive responsibly and with consideration for others? If not, why not? (CCC 2290).
Confess the answer and examples.

Do I make positive contributions to the community? If not, why not? (CCC 2235-43, 2255-56).
Confess the answer.

Do I take my vocation seriously and live up to my responsibilities? If not, why not?
(CCC 2427-28, 1604).
Confess the answer.

My relationship
with myself

Ask yourself and the Lord:

Do I feel angry often? (CCC 2259, 2262, 2302).
If so, is it because I expect everything and everyone to march to my beat? Am I acting as though I were God?
If so, confess it and examples of playing God.

Do I accept that the Father loves me?
If not, why not?
Confess the answer.

Am I seeking to know God's will so that I may consent and cooperate? If not, why not?
Confess the answer.

Am I unwilling or afraid to say "Yes" to God?
If so, why?
Confess the answer.

Do I prefer my own plans?
If so, confess this.

Do I cherish and care for my body as the gift of God? If not, why not? (CCC 364-65).
Confess the answer and instances.

Have I been greedy, lustful, or lazy? If so, why? (CCC 1866).
Confess the answer and the self-indulgence.

Do I live by the pleasure principle: "I want what I want when I want it" in any area of my life?
Confess the answer.

Human freedom (CCC 908, 1730-48)

Am I the prisoner of fear, anxiety, worry, guilt, inferiority, hatred of myself? Do I hand over the past to God's merciful love?
Do I allow it to trouble me still?
Hand these over to the Lord again and again, and he will set you free.

Do I plan prudently for future things that are within my choice and control and hand the rest to God's wise love?
Do I fret with worry, anticipating what might happen?
Hand these over to the Lord again and again, and he will set you free.

In the presence of our Lord, ask him to let you see yourself as he sees you. He loves you so much that he laid down his life for you.

Always look at your dark side only through the eyes of Jesus your savior, your healer, your brother, your shepherd, your lord.

Recall the words of Jesus to the woman accused of adultery, "Neither do I condemn you" (John 8:11). Since God acquits you, who are you to condemn yourself?

Now rest in his presence and be still.

If you have written your answers, read over and reflect on what you have found from our Lord and his Spirit.

Ask the Blessed Virgin Mary for her help

(CCC 148-49, 721-26, 2673-79, 2682).

The sacrament

(CCC 1450-60)

When the time comes,
with Mary praying with you and for you,
go to meet our Lord Jesus in the sacrament
of his forgiveness.

- Confess your sins
- Express your sorrow
- Receive absolution
- Experience freedom
- Accept healing
- Recognize the grace to grow in love

Enter once more into the still center
of yourself.
Become aware of Jesus there.
Give thanks to him.

Through him and with him give thanks to the Father and to the Holy Spirit.

Ask Mary to give thanks with you.

Make your penance a part of your thanksgiving.

As you go out,
Jesus goes with you—wherever you go—
with his gift of peace,
so that you may grow in love
and be an instrument of his peace—
wherever you are.

Times and seasons

In Advent, the liturgy of the Church is concerned with those areas of our life that are still closed to the Lord. We can examine these areas as preparation for our Christmas celebration of the sacrament.

In Lent, the liturgy is concerned with repentance and renewal through the death and resurrection of the Lord. Therefore we examine these areas as we prepare for our Easter celebration of the sacrament.

At Pentecost, the liturgy celebrates the gift of the Spirit for the forgiveness of our sins. We can meditate on this as we prepare for this season's celebration of the sacrament.

The Church's year ends with the feast of Christ the King. We can review all areas of our life at that time, saying "Thy Kingdom come" as we prepare again for a celebration of the sacrament.

Surrender

Gradually you will open your whole self to the Lord, not keeping any rooms in you locked or closed off to him. Let Jesus take over. Your willingness to let the Lord direct your daily life releases his saving power in you. Make a gift of yourself to him. Surrender your life and your love to him.